A Biblical ECONOMICS Manifesto

CREATION HOUSE

James P. Gills, M.D.
Ronald H. Nash, Ph.D.

A BIBLICAL ECONOMICS MANIFESTO
by James P. Gills, M.D., and Ronald H. Nash, Ph.D.
Published by Creation House
A Part of Charisma Media
600 Rinehart Road
Lake Mary, Florida 32746
www.charismamedia.com

Unless otherwise noted, Scripture quotations are from
The Holy Bible, New International Version, © 1973, 1978, 1984
by the International Bible Society. Used by permission of
Zondervan Publishing House. All rights reserved.

Scripture quotations marked KJV are from
the King James Version of the Bible.

Library of Congress Control Number: 2002100152
International Standard Book Number: 978-0-88419-871-0

E-book International Standard Book Number: 978-1-59979-925-4

11 12 13 14 — 8 7 6 5 4

Printed in the United States of America

DEDICATION

This book is dedicated to the leaders of America in business and politics who have given themselves to others, and to all the people of this country who are constantly **giving so much** back to their communities. If more gave of themselves, we would have no need for Big Government.

Freedom and responsibility are the twin ingredients for fulfillment and productivity in our personal lives (spiritual, mental, and physical) and in our society as a whole. Dr. Gills' book *Imaginations...More Than You Think* points out that we are responsible not only for what we do, but also for what we think. We must be responsible; then we can be free! The purpose of life is to love a purposeful life—to be ennobled steward-servants.

ACKNOWLEDGMENT

Gus Stavros is a successful entrepreneur, businessman, and generous philanthropist who has been dedicated to economic education since the 1970s. He also is a valued friend. "There's no free lunch" is a summary of Gus' approach to economic teaching and theory that is an integral part of this book.

TABLE OF CONTENTS

PREFACE

As I grew up in Bluefield, West Virginia, my father worked for American Electric Power. His territory bordered the Tennessee Valley Authority, a New Deal project intended to bring electricity to the people of the region. My dad was constantly challenged because he would build power lines down a country road to serve his rural people, and the TVA would come beside him and build its own power lines. The TVA was putting in those lines with the government's money and selling electricity for half his price, even though it cost the agency twice as much to make it.

My father also was the head of regional development, bringing industry to the southwestern part of Virginia. When industry became interested in an area, the TVA would come and offer a free site and free electricity for a period of time. But the money behind its offer came from taxes paid by people from all over the United States. Many of these taxpayers earned the money they used to pay their taxes by working for private industries that were being put out of business by the TVA. Even as a young man, I realized this was unfair. The supposedly compassionate government was putting honest businessmen and businesswomen out of work! Under the guise of helping some people, the government was doing enormous harm to others.

Back then, many Americans believed the government that governs least governs best. Over the years, millions of

Americans have been duped into thinking that none of us can survive without government help from the cradle to the grave, from the womb to the tomb. During the past few decades, most Americans have paid an enormous price in lost liberties and vastly increased taxes. As government has intruded into areas of life never anticipated nor condoned by the Founding Fathers, the increasing concentration of power in the federal government continues to produce serious failings throughout such areas of American society as education,[1] the economy,[2] and healthcare.[3] During the presidential election of 2000, it was shockingly obvious how many Americans had little concern about the inefficiencies in our government and so much indifference about the untruthful ways in which political arguments were presented. Equally bad, in my view, were the ways in which untrue political claims produced resentment and distrust between different groups of people. And I saw how socialist thinking continues to creep into our economic system.

In our earlier book *Government Is Too Big*, Dr. Ronald H. Nash and I dealt with many of these problems. This time, I thought, we ought to focus our attention on the widespread misinformation about so many fundamental issues in economics. When it comes to economics, as in many other areas, what you don't know *can* hurt you.

My coauthor, Dr. Nash, often refers to economics as the missing link in the Christian worldview. For many, economics is still a region of mystery. We do not believe this has to be the case. Our purpose in this book is to provide a simple, clear, and competent introduction to several fundamental areas of economics. It is also our purpose to do this in a way that is faithful to the Christian worldview.

There is another important reason for our writing. As more Americans become more dependent upon Big Government, they become more reluctant to assume responsibility for their own actions. Like Esau in the Old Testament, they are trading their birthright of liberty and independence for a mess of Big Government pottage. We need to get away from a governmental bureaucracy that controls so many aspects of our lives. We need to recover the lost sense of responsibility and stop looking to government as the solution to our problems. Such a government does not offer solutions; it only keeps creating new problems that will continue to lead us down the path to servitude and bondage.

As Americans, we need and deserve a smaller, more efficient government. We need to rediscover and celebrate the freedom we have to make decisions and accept the responsibility that comes with that freedom. Only then can we be truly free; only then can we truly prosper.

—James P. Gills, M.D.

CHAPTER 1

LAYING A FOUNDATION

Many pundits have said the close vote in the recent presidential election showed a great divide in this country: Half of us are liberals, and half are conservatives. They say we are a divided nation.

The real explanation is not that simple. The election results more accurately depict the ability of politicians to muddy the waters about the issues we hold dear—our basic beliefs, morals, and values. Politicians have tried to mislead our thinking about individual rights and responsibilities, as well as how we view the role of government in our lives. We are not divided; we are confused. We've lost sight of our basic belief in the free market and have become convinced government has a right to control increasingly large segments of our economic activity.

Even worse, some powerful people in America seem to be engaged in promoting class warfare, trying to pit rich against poor, the powerful against the powerless. As Texas Senator Phil Gramm has said so well, the only bigotry that is now socially acceptable is bigotry against the successful. Numbers of poor and powerless people in our nation have been deceived into voting against their own interests by powerful people, many of them politicians, whose real purpose is to maintain or expand their own power. One of the more important contributing factors to this situation is confusion about some fundamental concepts of economics.

The mere mention of economics frightens or intimidates some people. They think the subject of economics is too difficult for most of us to understand. We disagree, and through the following pages, we hope to make important aspects of economics simple and easy to understand. Jesus Himself taught the importance of being able to think about economic issues. In Luke 14:28, Jesus said, "Suppose one of you wants to build a tower. Will he not first sit down and estimate the cost to see if he has enough money to complete it?"

We believe it is important for Christians to think more clearly about the economic options. We want to examine how false, misleading, and deceptive theories about economics are turning many Americans into socialists without their comprehending what is really happening. But before this can be done, all of us need a better understanding of the differences between socialism and the free market alternative.

CONFUSED CHRISTIANS

One of the more regrettable features of this economic confusion is its spread into the thinking of many Christians. A number of Christians these days show little regard for capitalism. They think capitalism is supposed to be non-Christian or anti-Christian because it allegedly gives a predominant place to greed and other non-Christian values. Capitalism is alleged to increase poverty and the misery of the poor while making a few rich at the expense of the many. Socialism, on the other hand, is portrayed as the economic system of people who really care for the less fortunate members of society. Socialism is represented as the economics of compassion. Some writers have gone so far as to claim that socialism is an essential part of the Christian gospel.[4]

In one of his writings, Dr. Nash talks about the two faces of Christian compassion for the poor.[5] Many Christians have come to recognize that they have an obligation to be concerned about more than the condition of their neighbor's soul. Such Christians understand their duty is to be concerned about the plight of the poor, about social injustice, about urban blight, and about other issues of social significance.

As important as the social concern of the contemporary Christian may be, it is only one side of the story. A Christian does have a clear obligation to care and to be concerned about the poor and oppressed and to do what he can on their behalf. But the other dimension of Christian social concern adds the stipulation that if a Christian wishes to make pronouncements on complex social, economic, and political issues, he also has a duty to become informed about these issues, including economics.

Unfortunately, many Christian social activists manifest an inadequate grasp of economics. The late Benjamin Rogge, a professor of economics and Lutheran layman, lamented that "the typical American who calls himself a Christian and who makes pronouncements...on economic policies or institutions, does so out of an almost complete ignorance of the simplest and most widely accepted tools of economic analysis. If something arouses his Christian concern, he asks not whether it is water or gasoline he is tossing on the economic fire—he asks only whether it is a well-intended act. As I understand it, the Christian is required to use his God-given reason as well."[6]

Few Christians have made the effort to study the foundational issues that underlie the problems of poverty and social justice. It is not enough to feel compassion for the poor and oppressed. Compassion and love must be coupled with a careful grounding in the relevant philosophical, economic, political, and social issues.

Another reason why some attention to economics is important is the clear evidence that many attempts to help the poor in America in the past forty years have had precisely the opposite effect. When "aid" for the poor is grounded on bad economics, it usually will make any bad situation worse. A large number of books about social justice that have appeared since 1960 have been authored by writers who reject and condemn political and economic conservatism as a cruel, heartless, and uncaring movement totally out of step with an informed biblical view. Many such writers insist that the Christian's undisputed obligation to demonstrate love for the needy obliges him to adopt politically liberal means to aid the poor, which leads inevitably to huge increases in the size and power of government.[7] While politically liberal Christians may deserve praise for their compassion, the means they adopt to help the poor have done significantly more harm than good.

THE ECONOMIC WAY OF THINKING

One relatively simple way to approach economics for the first time is through a tool sometimes called "the economic way of thinking." Some economists have pointed out the value of viewing economics not so much as a set of doctrines or conclusions, but as a distinctive way of thinking. The principles that underlie the economic way of thinking are not difficult to grasp; they are often matters of common sense. But anyone who is

unaware of these principles will have difficulty understanding the facts of economics.

THE IMPORTANCE OF INCENTIVES

The economic way of thinking begins by recognizing the
importance of incentives. The greater the benefits people
expect to receive from an alternative, the more people
are likely to choose that option. The greater the costs
expected from an alternative, the fewer people are likely
to select it.

If we understand what makes human beings tick, we can
make general predictions as to how individuals or groups
of individuals will respond to changes in their economic
situation—in particular, how they will respond to new
incentives. If a society establishes programs that provide
unemployed people with cash and noncash benefits that
approximate or even exceed what they would earn working (after taxes), one can safely predict that many of these
people will choose to remain unemployed. (Notice the
devastating effect this choice will have on people's sense
of responsibility for their own well-being.) If a welfare
program is set up in such a way that it provides incentives for unmarried women who become pregnant to
remain unmarried, we should not be surprised when the
rate of illegitimate births begins to increase. (Once again,
notice the evil consequences this has for individual human
responsibility.)

In economics, you get what you pay for. If you give people incentives to do A rather than B, the number of people
who choose A—all other things being equal—will increase.
The truth is that many facets of liberal welfare programs
have given people bad incentives and have therefore produced bad consequences.

Because human beings live in a world marked by scarcity, nothing is free. Every economic good has a price in the sense that before anyone can obtain it, something else must be sacrificed. It is impossible to get A (some economic good) without giving up B (some other economic good). The economic principle in view here is often expressed in such sayings as, "You can't have your cake and eat it, too," and "There is no such thing as a free lunch." The unavoidable fact of scarcity in life forces us to make choices in which we sacrifice some things in order to obtain others. When Big Government forcibly takes from some people (via taxation) and gives to others, it is easy for the recipients of the largesse of Big Government to think that some goods and services, such as healthcare and prescription medicines, have no cost. The costs are still there, but the people who pay those costs often are out of sight and mind for those who not only take the results of government's redistribution of property but begin to act as though they are entitled to an increasing amount of such benefits. Once again, consider the negative effect such a process has upon individual responsibility.

SCARCITY, CHOICE, AND PERSONAL VALUE

In a world of scarcity, choice and sacrifice are unavoidable. People's economic behavior is simply a reflection of, first, their need to make choices, and, second, the relative value they place upon their options. In cases where it is impossible for someone to have both A and B, the choice a person makes will reflect the relative value he places upon A and B. People's actions, then, reflect their value scales. Their choices are made in order to help them secure the alternatives that fit more closely with their values.

The value that different people place upon different economic goods varies from person to person. People's value scales are personal and different. One person might prefer to spend an hour watching a baseball game on TV, while someone else might choose to watch a classic movie or a cooking show. Still another person might prefer to read a book or play chess. It would be highly unusual ever to find two people who ranked every economic good in precisely the same way.

ECONOMIC UNCERTAINTY

We seldom know enough about individuals, even people especially close to us, to predict with total certainty what choices they will make among various economic goods. We may know that a particular friend ranks tickets to Chicago Cubs baseball games very highly in his personal scale of values. But we may not know how smitten he has become with the young lady he met yesterday and how, suddenly, the prospect of a picnic at the beach with his new friend has become more important than watching the Cubs play the Cardinals. Human value scales are more than intensely personal; they are always changing. Because people's economic choices reflect their ever-changing value scales, predictions about human economic choices will always be characterized by uncertainty. This uncertainty plays a major role in the unpredictability of business ventures. It also explains why overzealous politicians or even economists cannot predict the future of governmental intervention with the operations of a free market.

THE IMPORTANCE OF LONG-RANGE CONSEQUENCES

We can test the success of economic theories in predicting and explaining what takes place in the real world. One way of assessing any economic proposal is to ask what its long-range consequences will be. It is a mistake to notice only the short-run or immediate consequences of economic activity. Any proposal or policy can affect the way people view a situation and thus can alter their incentives in ways that change their choices. Such a change in incentives often produces other effects that become noticeable only in the long run.

Many economic policies have been enacted because they appeared to produce desired consequences in the short run. This has often been true of policies designed to help the less fortunate people in society. But measures that appeared beneficial when viewed in the short term often look quite different after a few years. One reason this happens is because the policies produce incentives that lead people to modify their behavior in ways that turn the short-run success into a long-term disaster.

Human behavior frequently has unintended consequences. Even compassionate acts can have unintended consequences. Suppose the government passes laws that make it difficult to fire employees. While that might sound good to some, what if such laws also discourage businesses from hiring employees? What if laws that increase the penalties for sexual assault result in the criminal being more likely to murder his victim? What if America's distribution of free food to certain countries discourages local farming?

Several years ago, a politically liberal Christian author named Ronald Sider argued that Americans should unilaterally begin to pay more than a market price for certain commodities from poor countries.[8] Sider seemed blissfully unaware of the long-range consequences such policies would have on the economy of poorer nations. But such economic shortsightedness did not escape the attention of

George Mavrodes, a University of Michigan philosopher, who wrote: "Sider seems unaware that his policies may have different results than he intends. Suppose that we [Americans] voluntarily increased the price that we pay for crude rubber (a recurrent suggestion of Sider's), then, Sider says, rubber workers would get higher wages. Fine. But wouldn't rubber producers scramble to increase production? And wouldn't land and labor be diverted from other enterprises, such as food production, to cash in on higher rubber prices? Since we don't need more rubber, the increased production would represent a waste of resources. Sider seems not to notice such consequences."[9]

Many recent proposals made in the name of Christian compassion or "Christian economics" are bad economics in the sense that over the long run, they are counterproductive. A number of important books document the claim that antipoverty programs in the United States have actually increased poverty.[10] According to economist James Gwartney, "Seeking to promote the welfare of the poor, the disadvantaged, the unemployed, and the misfortunate, well-meaning citizens (including a good many evangelical Christians) have inadvertently supported forms of economic organization that have promoted the precise outcomes they sought to alleviate. For too long, socially concerned Christians have measured policies by the intentions of their advocates, rather than the predictable effectiveness of the programs. Put simply, in our haste to do something constructive, we have not thought very seriously about the impact, particularly in the long run, of alternative policies on the well-being of the intended beneficiaries."[11]

Gwartney's quote is only one statement of many in which economists allege that America's welfare programs of the recent past contradict several basic principles of the economic way of thinking.

Many programs to help the poor are like heroin addiction. The unfortunate person who begins to experiment with the drug feels immediate satisfaction. A want he may not have known before is satisfied in ways he may not have thought possible. But while the newly found want fosters the need for continuing satisfaction, the drug begins to take control. Soon the person cannot function without the drug; he has become an addict. In a similar way, various programs to help the poor may seem to provide some immediate relief. But as soon as people see what the new rules are, they change their behavior to reflect the new incentives or disincentives. When the unfortunate long-term effects of the policy finally become recognizable, it is often too late. Too many people are hooked; they are victims of a new kind of slavery. Any threat to such policies as "affirmative action," free medical care, free prescription drugs, or automatic admission to a college regardless of grades and test scores is viewed with the same dread the addict has when his supply of heroin is threatened. The possibility that a decrease in tax transfers might give people new incentives to become more self-reliant and more responsible is often drowned in a sea of rhetoric about "compassion."

Minimum wage legislation is another example of conflict with the economic way of thinking. Minimum wage laws are justified as actions that will help low-skilled workers earn more money. However, such laws only force employers to lay off a greater number of unskilled workers because many do not have ability commensurate with the level of the minimum wage. The law that was supposed to help unskilled workers earn more money has the long-range effect of making many of them unemployed.

CONCLUSION

Sound economics will always accord with the guide-posts of the economic way of thinking. When Christians begin to tout specific economic views or policies, they should be careful to examine them in the light of these principles. Real power for the people of this great country comes from understanding these economic concepts and taking the responsibility for applying those concepts in our lives. Armed with such knowledge, we have the power, through the voting booth and beyond, to transform the way American government operates.

In a free market, individuals—and not the government—determine the value of goods and services. In such a system, when individuals are accountable and responsible for their decisions, people are enabled to make the best transactions that benefit themselves. This is one of the greatest benefits of a free market system. This freedom is why many people have come to the United States. We need to return to the ideals of a free market system and work to challenge the socialist thinking that has changed the face of American government.

CHAPTER 2

"WE WANT A KING"

We have argued that many false, misleading, and deceptive theories about economics are turning many Americans into socialists without their knowing it. These people uncritically surrender to such socialist attacks on the free market system as the following: Capitalism makes a few people rich at the expense of many; capitalism increases poverty and the misery of the poor.

We disagree. We suggest that people should be given freedom, with minimal regulation, to pursue their goals. Only then will people have the greatest opportunity for prosperity and satisfaction. A socialist government actually decreases the people's standard of living.[12]

The primary purpose of government is to protect the freedom of its citizens. When politicians overreach and overregulate, the health of the country's economy suffers. Government becomes inefficient and intrudes into the lives of citizens. The last century provided dramatic examples of that in China, Cuba, North Korea, and in the former Soviet Union and its totalitarian allies in Eastern Europe.

SAMUEL SPEAKS

The Bible offers an important lesson about the struggle

between the people and governmental bureaucracy. In the Old Testament, after the time of Joshua, the Israelites anxiously asked: "Who will deliver us from the Philistines?" They wanted to overthrow the ungodly Philistines who were oppressing the Israelites. In answer to their prayer, God raised up Samuel, a great judge and prophet. He resolved the disputes between the tribes of Israel and spoke the word of God clearly and eloquently.

Chapter 7 of the Book of I Samuel tells us how the Philistines surrounded the Israelites. The people pleaded with Samuel, "Do not stop crying out to the LORD our God for us, that he may rescue us from the hand of the Philistines" (I Sam. 7:8). They were delivered. The Israelites routed the Philistines, and Samuel praised God, saying, "Thus far has the LORD helped us" (v. 12). Samuel also took a stone and made a memorial, calling it Ebenezer. *Eben* means "stone"; *ezer* means "help." This Ebenezer was a reminder for the Israelites to live by gratitude and responsibility.

For many years, Samuel led the people of Israel wisely and with the authority of the Lord. As he grew old, however, the people could see that his sons would not rule as well. Rather than relying on God's provision to raise up a new leader, they sought a solution of their own. The question before them was whether they wanted to continue in faithful dependence on God. Sadly, their answer was no.

> So all the elders of Israel gathered together and came to Samuel at Ramah. They said to him, "You are old, and your sons do not walk in your ways; now appoint a king to lead us, such as all the other nations have."
>
> —I SAMUEL 8:4–5

The Israelites feared the future and rejected the trust they had placed in God's provision. They wanted a king to raise an army and fight their battles, rather than calling on God to send a deliverer. God replied to Samuel, "It is not you they have rejected, but they have rejected me as their king... Now listen to them; but warn them solemnly and let them know what the king who will reign over them will do" (1 Sam. 8:7, 9).

Here is God's warning to them through the prophet Samuel:

This is what the king who will reign over you will do: He will take your sons and make them serve with his chariots and horses... He will take your daughters to be perfumers and cooks and bakers. He will take the best of your fields and vineyards and olive groves and give them to his attendants. He will take a tenth of your grain and of your vintage and give it to his officials and attendants... The best of your cattle and donkeys he will take for his own use. He will take a tenth of your flocks, and you yourselves will become his slaves. When that day comes, you will cry out for relief from the king you have chosen, and the Lord will not answer you in that day.

—1 SAMUEL 8:11–18

They heard in no uncertain terms that choosing a ruler would come with great personal cost. A king would establish a bureaucracy, force their sons to serve in the army, take children away from families, and impose excessive taxes, thereby reducing their wealth. Samuel urged the Israelites to realize that they would lose their freedom and their prosperity if they chose a king.

Did the people heed God's warning through Samuel? Sadly, they did not. Their desire for security was greater than their desire for God. Listen to their response:

*"No!" they said. "We want a king over us. Then we will be like
all the other nations, with a king to lead us and to go out before
us and fight our battles."*

—1 SAMUEL 8:19–20

And so Saul became king of Israel. But he did not look
to God for wisdom in ruling the people; he looked to himself. He was followed by David, anointed by God as king
and a man after God's own heart. Yet David's success at
turning the tribes of Israel into a great nation was followed
by a staggering fall from power. The kingdom of Israel was
eventually defeated and divided up, and the Israelites were
taken into captivity.

The Israelites chose to trust in organization rather than
in God. While they didn't want to be oppressed by the
Philistines, they ended up suffering under the oppression
of their own central government. They paid higher taxes
to support a king and his court. Their sons and daughters
were taken away to serve the king. The family unit was
destroyed, along with the relationships of family and society. They didn't want the responsibility of making their
own choices.

The people of Israel thought they could get something
for nothing. They thought the security and protection of
a king would be free and easier for them. Instead, they
suffered under oppressive taxes, their social order was
destroyed, and their kingdom was demolished. Their choice
and their lack of personal responsibility cost them dearly.

The same is true for us today. Many people still want
something for nothing. They seek the security of a government that will provide for them, yet they do not see
what it has cost them. Our quality of life has suffered
under the strong bureaucracy that exists in Washington

today. Each of us pays more taxes than necessary to support an inefficient government. Fewer than twenty-five cents of every welfare dollar actually reaches the poor. The other seventy-five cents goes to pay for the huge bureaucracy. Money that should be used to support our families is siphoned off to sustain the bureaucracy—today's version of a king and his court. Our quality of life suffers. Government makes the rules and calls the shots; it interferes with parents' control over their families.

We pay an extremely high price for a lower standard of living. As we learned earlier, there is no such thing as a free lunch. We have paid dearly for an inefficient and domineering bureaucracy. Tragically, our desire for security has cost us our liberty.

No matter what people we respect believe, we need to listen to what the Bible says in I Samuel 8. We need to stop and think through the consequences of an economy controlled by government. God told the Israelites a king would come at great cost. It's the same with us today. Our modern version of a king—the bureaucracy—costs us our standard of living and limits our freedom. Even worse, its alleged compassion for the poor has pursued policies that have increased the number and misery of the poor.

CHAPTER 3

THE TWO MEANS OF EXCHANGE

The time has come for us to explain the major differences between socialism and capitalism. Unfortunately, many discussions of capitalism and socialism are unclear or just plain wrong. There is enormous confusion about the nature of these two systems. Many businessmen and women who may think of themselves as capitalists are really supporters of governmental controls that are, in fact, major steps in the direction of socialism.

We have found that the best and clearest way to explain the differences between capitalism and socialism is to begin by first distinguishing between the peaceful and violent means of exchange. This distinction refers to the only two ways in which anything can be exchanged.

THE PEACEFUL MEANS OF EXCHANGE

The peaceful means of exchange can be summed up in the phrase, "If you do something good for me, then I'll do something good for you." When I walk into a restaurant and place my order, I am using the peaceful means of exchange. In effect, I am saying that if you (waiter or waitress) do something good for me (serve me the food I have ordered), I will do something good for you (give you the money your employer charges for this product and give you a tip). The same process occurs when I buy a car or rent an apartment. One easy way to see the peaceful means of exchange at work is to visit a garage sale. Obviously there are times when the seller would prefer a higher price for the item he has for sale and the buyer might prefer a lower price. When the buyer and seller finally reach an agreement, their transaction illustrates the peaceful means of exchange.

When capitalism is understood correctly, it epitomizes the peaceful means of exchange. The reason people enter market exchanges is because they believe the exchange is good for them. They take advantage of an opportunity to obtain something they want more in exchange for something they value less. When people enter into voluntary transactions, when they utilize the peaceful means of exchange, their deeds enhance the welfare of others and enhance society's welfare. Both parties in voluntary exchanges benefit. Capitalism then should be understood as a voluntary system of relationships that utilizes the peaceful means of exchange.

THE VIOLENT MEANS OF EXCHANGE

Exchange can also take place by means of force and violence. In this violent means of exchange, the basic rule of thumb is, "Unless you do something good for me, I'll do something bad to you." This is the way thieves and crooks operate. It is also the way governments secure their revenue.

The violent means of exchange exemplifies the controlling principle of socialism. Socialism means far more than centralized control of the economic process. It entails the introduction of coercion into an economic exchange in order to facilitate the goals of powerful elitists who function as the central planners.

SOME COMMENTS ABOUT
"CHRISTIAN SOCIALISM"

We live in a day when many Christians promote what they call "Christian socialism."[13] Advocates of this view often appeal to Acts 4:32–35 in support of their position. In the language of the King James Version, these verses report that the early Christians in Jerusalem held all their possessions in common (v. 32) and these common goods were distributed "unto every man according as he had need" (v. 35).

But the actions described in Acts 4 are not instances of socialism. A free market system is not opposed to groups of people pooling their resources as long as they do it voluntarily, as members of the Jerusalem church did. A group of Christians freely pooling their resources temporarily in a time of need does not constitute socialism. In order for socialism to exist, there must be governmental coercion that forces people to behave in a certain way. This state-sponsored coercion cannot be found in Acts 4.

One of the great ironies of "Christian" socialism is that its proponents, in effect, demand that the state get out its weapons and force people to fulfill the demands of Christian love. Even if we fail to notice any other contrast between capitalism and socialism, we already have at least one major difference to relate to the biblical ethic. One system (capitalism) stresses voluntary and peaceful exchange while the other (socialism) depends on coercion and violence.

Some Christian Socialists object to the way we have framed the Christian debate over capitalism and socialism.

They profess contempt for the more coercive forms of state socialism as found in Cuba, North Korea, the People's Republic of China, and the former Soviet Union. They would like us to believe that a more humane, non-coercive kind of socialism is possible. They would like us to believe that there is a form of socialism not yet tried anywhere on earth, where the central ideas are cooperation and community and where coercion and dictatorship are precluded.

It is interesting to note how little information they provide about the workings of their utopian kind of socialism. They ignore the fact that however humane and voluntary their socialism is supposed to become after it has been put into effect, it will take massive amounts of coercion and theft to get it started. They are unable to explain how their system will work without free markets, and they simply ignore the coercion that will be required to get their system started. Whatever else socialism is, it means a centralized control of the economy made possible by the use of force. Socialism epitomizes the violent means of exchange. Voluntary socialism is a contradiction in terms.

How can so many church leaders and intellectuals insist that socialism is the only economic system compatible with Christianity? As writers such as Paul Hollander point out, socialism has definite snob appeal among the intellectual elite. Many people think it is chic to be a socialist. According to Hollander:

> The appeals and values associated with socialism ... have provided the most powerful incentive for the suspension of critical thinking among large contingents of Western intellectuals ... Such intellectuals appear to assume an affirming, supportive stance as soon as a political system (or movement) makes an insistent enough claim to its socialist character ... The word

"socialism" has retained, despite all historical disappointments associated with regimes calling themselves socialist, a certain magic which rarely fails to disarm or charm these intellectuals and which inspires renewed hope that its most recent incarnation will be the authentic one, or at least more authentic than previous ones had been.[14]

Of course, Hollander continues, "There is little evidence that intellectuals, or for that matter non-intellectuals, living in countries considered Socialist are similarly charmed or disarmed by the idea of socialism."[15] Professor Benjamin Rogge was one economist who understood the folly of any so-called Christian socialism. As he put it, "The Christian who enthusiastically embraces coercive, collective charity may very possibly be deriving his mandate from some source other than his own religion...Today's Christian economics seems to me to be neither good Christianity nor good economics."

A CLOSER LOOK AT CAPITALISM

We have already explained capitalism as a system of voluntary human relationships in which people exchange on the basis of the peaceful means of exchange. It is time to add more detail to this general picture. For one thing, capitalism is not economic anarchy. It recognizes several necessary conditions for the kinds of voluntary relationships it recommends. One of these is the existence of inherent human rights, such as the right to make decisions, the right to be free, the right to hold property, and the right to exchange what one owns for something else. Capitalism also presupposes a system of morality. Capitalism does not encourage people to do anything they want. There are definite limits, moral and otherwise, to the ways in which people should exchange. Capitalism should be regarded as a system of voluntary relationships within a framework of laws that protect people's rights against force, fraud, theft, and violations of contracts. "Thou shalt not steal" and "Thou shalt not lie" are part of the underlying moral constraints of the system. Economic exchanges can hardly be voluntary if one participant is coerced, deceived, defrauded, or robbed.

When people exchange freely, their actions promote economic progress. Mutual gain is the foundation of economic exchange. People enter into economic exchanges because they believe they will benefit or gain something. "If you do something good for me, then I'll do something good for you." Free economic exchange is productive because each participant in the trade gets more of what he wants.

Free economic exchanges move economic goods to people who value them the most. In this way, something that is largely worthless to one person is traded to another person who prizes it greatly. Following such a trade, the wealth of both people is increased. Voluntary exchange is productive because it promotes social cooperation and helps us get more of what we want. People derive income from helping others. The best way to increase your income honestly is to find better ways to help other people.

CAPITALISM, SOCIALISM, AND THE PROBLEM OF HUMAN SIN

There is no mystery as to why existing economic systems fall short of the capitalist ideal. The reason is implicit in one of the major tenets of the Christian worldview. Deviations from the market ideal often occur because of defects in human nature. Human beings naturally crave security and guaranteed success, values not found readily in a free market. Genuine competition always carries with it the possibility of failure and loss. Consequently, the understandable human preference for security leads humans to avoid competition whenever possible, encourages them to operate outside of the market and induces them to subvert the market process through behavior that is often questionable and dishonest. As long as the human beings taking part in market exchanges are sinners, we should expect to find problems.

One of the sillier objections to capitalism is the claim that it presupposes a utopian view of human nature. Our earlier statement about the need for laws to protect people from force, fraud, and theft hardly sounds as though capitalism is unaware of the true condition of human nature. In fact, once we grant that consistency with the biblical doctrine of sin is a legitimate test of economic systems, it is relatively easy to see how well democratic capitalism scores in this regard.

One of the more effective ways of mitigating the effects of human sin in society is dispersing and decentralizing power. The combination of a free market economy and limited constitutional government is the most effective means yet devised to impede the concentration of economic and political power in the hands of a small number of people. Every person's ultimate protection against coercion requires control over some private spheres of life where he or she can be free. For example, private ownership of property is an important buffer against any exorbitant consolidation of power by government.

The free market is consistent with the biblical view of human nature in another way. It recognizes the weaknesses of human nature and the limitations of human knowledge. No one can possibly know enough to manage a complex economy. No one should ever be trusted with this power. This statement applies with equal force to people who control large corporations, to politicians who control a nation, and to the small group of appointed individuals who control the Federal Reserve System. In order for socialism to work, it requires a class of omniscient planners to forecast the future, to set prices, and to control production. In the free market system, decisions are not made by an omniscient bureaucratic elite, but made across the entire economic system by countless economic agents.

At this point, of course, critics of capitalism are quick to raise an objection. Capitalism, they will counter, may make it difficult for economic power to be consolidated in the hands of government; but it only makes it easier for vast concentrations of wealth and power to be vested in the hands of private individuals and companies. But the truth turns out to be something quite different from this widely accepted myth. It is not the free market that produces monopolies; rather it is government intervention with the market that creates the conditions that encourage monopoly. The only real monopolies that have attained a high degree of immunity from competition achieved that status by governmental fiat, regulation, or support of some other kind. Governments create monopolies by granting one organization the exclusive privilege of doing business or by establishing de facto monopolies through regulatory agencies whose alleged purpose is the enforcement of competition. However, the real effect of these agencies is the limitation of competition. More attention needs to be given to the ways in which America's infamous nineteenth-century "robber barons" were aided by special privileges granted by government.

SOME MAJOR WEAKNESSES
OF SOCIALISM

One dominant feature of capitalism is economic freedom, the right of people to exchange things voluntarily, free from force, fraud, and theft. Capitalism is more than this, of course, but its concern with free exchange is obvious. Socialism, on the other hand, seeks to replace the freedom of the market with a group of central planners who exercise control over essential market functions. There are degrees of socialism as there are degrees of capitalism in the real world. But basic to any form of socialism is distrust of or contempt for the market process and the desire to replace the freedom of the market with some form of centralized control.

The fundamental flaw in socialism was discovered around 1920 by an Austrian economist named Ludwig von Mises. Mises argued that socialism is not only undesirable; it turns out to be an economic system that makes rational economic behavior impossible. The reason is simple: Decisions about whether to buy a good or service require some indication of cost. Without an accurate barometer of how a person will end up after an exchange, one could not make a rational economic decision. The basic indicator that signals when people should or should not engage in an economic transaction is price. But we cannot have pricing information without markets. And real markets cannot exist in a socialist system.

To illustrate this, imagine someone who is a manager of a factory in the old Soviet Union. Let us suppose the factory manufactures widgets (a widget can be anything you want it to be). In a socialist system, the government owns the building, the machinery and tools in the factory, the equipment that supplies electricity, and the raw materials from which the widgets will be made. Even if we suppose the factory does a wonderful job of making lots of widgets, what price does it seek when the time comes to sell the widgets? It would be economic madness to sell widgets that cost, let us say, ten cents each for only five cents. But here's the catch for the socialist factory: Since under socialism the government owns everything, how can anyone know what it costs to make one widget? Any "costs" in such a system would be artificial, contrived, and phony.

One method the old Soviet Union used to get pricing information was to send spies to places such as the United States to see what products were selling for. Imagine a Soviet named Igor phoning Moscow to report that the Wal-Mart in St. Louis was selling widgets for nine cents apiece while Natasha called to say that the Kmart in Brooklyn was selling them for eight cents. Provided with this market information, the Soviets announced that they would sell widgets for seven cents. If not for pricing information supplied by capitalist economies, the old Soviet system would have collapsed long before it did.

Socialism is a fraudulent economic system that makes rational economic activity impossible. As early as 1920, Mises saw that production can never be attuned to human wants without markets to set prices. The impossibility of precise measures of cost accounting under socialism resulted in general impoverishment.[16]

Socialism is inferior to capitalism in a number of ways. One of them is the degree of efficiency. British economist Brian Griffiths explains: "The reason that private ownership encourages efficiency and growth is that the rewards from hard work, innovation, risk-takings, restructuring, and investment accrue to those who make the decisions...It is impossible to create similar incentives in nationalized industries to those which exist for business-men with equity interest in small firms."[17]

In other words, a market system provides important incentives that are missing from socialism. Under socialism, Griffiths continues, "Rewards are not related to effort and commercial risk-taking, but to party membership, bureau-cratic status, political fiat, and corruption. As a conse-quence, the legitimate commercial entrepreneurial spirit is killed; for perfectly understandable reasons, people devote their resources to hacking a way through the political and bureaucratic jungle of their economies."[18]

Socialism restricts wealth and creates poverty. As Winston Churchill once said, "The inherent vice of capital-ism is the unequal sharing of blessings; the inherent vice of socialism is the equal sharing of miseries." Instead of ask-ing why so many people are poor, the real question is how so many people escape from poverty. How have so many people, acting in ways that are not coercive and immoral, created wealth for themselves and others? How have so many people prospered even as they enriched the lives of so many others? Clearly, irrefutably, the answer to such questions can never be socialism.

CHAPTER 4

IS THERE A THIRD ECONOMIC OPTION?

Many people are attracted by the possibility of an economic system that would fall somewhere between capitalism and socialism, that might, they think, combine the best features of each. If we consider capitalism and socialism as opposite ends of a spectrum, somewhere in the middle is a third system that we call interventionism. Consider the following diagram:

Capitalism   **Interventionism**   **Socialism**

$$\longleftarrow\hspace{8cm}\longrightarrow$$

As the name suggests, interventionism is an economic system in which agents of governmental power think they have the right to intervene in or interfere with the operation of a market economy whenever it suits their plans for society. Interventionism results from the mistaken belief that governmental intervention in economic matters can successfully achieve desired results while still falling short of the total controls that characterize a socialist system. In reality, interventionism is a system in which government interferes with the normal operation of the market system in order to alter the terms of trade in ways that benefit some at the expense of others. Interventionism is a result of one group inviting government to enter the market process and change the rates at which exchanges take place.

Advocates of interventionism never explain that this is what their system really is. Instead, they talk in lofty moral terms about the importance of certain social goals and how those goals can only be attained if government intervenes in ways that will counterbalance the selfishness of some in order to bring about the good for all.

Recognizing the existence of interventionism is extremely important. For one thing, capitalism is often rejected or criticized because it is confused with interventionism. In truth, the economy of the United States these days is not a form of capitalism; it is a version of interventionism. Many complaints about the economic policies of the United States are justified. But when the programs and policies that cause problems result from interventionism, it is hardly fair to blame those problems on capitalism. This is especially true in the case of Third World nations that attack the so-called capitalism of the United States in order to justify their own nations' drift toward totalitarianism. While capitalism may well have problems of its own, it seems unfair to blame it for the problems caused by a different economic system—interventionism.

There is another reason it is important to distinguish between capitalism and interventionism. When interventionist measures lead, as they often do, to serious economic problems, interventionist economists and politicians never admit that the problems result from governmental tampering with the economy. The problems, they complain, result from the fact that there was insufficient governmental intervention in the economy. In this clever but dishonest way, the failures of interventionism are cited as reasons for even greater degrees of government interference with the economy. It is precisely this kind of government interventionism that started the Great Depression in 1929 and continued that Depression for more than a decade.[19]

An interventionist government uses such tools as wage and price controls, taxes, tariffs (taxes on imports) and manipulation of the money supply to work its will on the people. Increases in the money supply are the major cause of inflation. Between 1914, the year the Federal Reserve System began its work, and sometime in the 1990s, the continuing inflation of the American dollar passed 1,000 percent. This means that if in 1914 some person had hidden away $1,000, the purchasing power of that money would now equal less than $100. Someone or something effectively stole more than $900 from that family. The thief was the U.S. government. The theft was simply interventionism at work.

Interventionism controls and regulates money, controls production, raises the price of goods and services, controls wages, and supports certain businesses in specific areas of industry. With regard to the control of money, the biggest cause of all depressions was excessive tightening of money by the federal government. To recall points made in the Preface, the TVA spent twice as much to make a kilowatt hour as its competitors but didn't pay any taxes. It gave free electricity to favored industries in its areas, which led industries to move in from neighboring states. That benefited states in the TVA region but hurt states outside the area. This shows how interventionism alters the terms of trade to benefit some at the expense of others.

INTERVENTIONISM'S ACHILLES' HEEL

The basic failure of interventionism lies in the fact that no third alternative to a free market or socialism is possible. The partial governmental controls that are supposed to distinguish interventionism from the more total controls of a socialist system inevitably fail. Interference with market processes will not only fail to attain the government/interventionist's goals, but it will produce conditions worse than those it sought to alter through its controls. This is not to say that things may not appear better in the short run. But in the long run, the unforeseen consequences will be worse than if the interventionist had done nothing at all.

Imagine that our government decides that the price of eggs is too high. Because it wants to make it easier for poor people to buy eggs, the bureaucrats decide that the imposition of controls on the price of eggs will benefit the poor. Liberals find it easy to congratulate themselves for their humanitarianism and condemn the greedy business people who are too interested in making a profit to care that a basic human need is unmet. Because the government cares, it will now act to alleviate that need.

Suppose that the market price for eggs is a dollar a dozen and that the politicians decide that the quickest way to make eggs more easily available to the poor is to pass a law making it illegal to retail eggs for more than seventy-five cents a dozen. As soon as the ceiling price drops below the market price of one dollar, all kinds of unforeseen consequences will occur. First of all, marginal egg producers will find that they are losing money. In every case where a producer's costs (for chicken feed, electricity, gasoline, and so on) exceed his profit under the newly imposed price ceiling, the government's interference will result in some egg producers leaving the market. Rather than continue to lose money, many marginal producers will probably sell their chickens to Kentucky Fried Chicken and find something more profitable to do. Perhaps they will even give up farming when they discover they can do just as well on welfare.

After the government-imposed price ceiling forces many marginal farmers out of the egg business, fewer eggs will be available, a result that is precisely the opposite of what the bureaucrats originally intended. The politicians believed that their intervention into the market would make eggs more available. But as things turned out, their action only made eggs more scarce. At this point, the politicians have two choices. They might decide to regulate prices all the way down the line. That is, they might decide that they can retain the price ceiling on eggs and still keep marginal producers in the egg market by imposing additional controls on the major costs of the chicken farmer. If the marginal chicken farmer cannot stay in business because of the high cost of grain, the way to solve that problem is to impose new price controls on chicken feed.

But this simply pushes the problem back to the level of the grain farmer. If he cannot make a profit growing grain, he will turn to something else, which will have the effect of making grain more scarce. It soon becomes obvious that the only way governmental intervention into the market can succeed is if it exercises total control. But this, of course, would be socialism and mark an end to any experiment in a mixed economy. What began presumably as an innocent, humane, benevolent (and foolish) governmental attempt to make eggs available to more people at a lower price has not only failed, but has also introduced total state control over an entire industry.

The other choice for the interventionist politicians is to admit the mistake and end the controls. Naturally, the removal of controls will produce a number of problems until the disastrous effects of the intervention are gradually overcome through the ordinary processes of the market.

In the case of controls on the price of eggs, a removal of the ceiling price in conjunction with the government-induced shortage will result in a dramatic but temporary rise in the price of eggs. The higher price, for which the government is responsible, will cause hardship among the poor people whom liberal politicians were supposedly trying to help. But the higher price will also be a signal to new producers that this is now a good time to enter the egg business. Eventually, the increased supply will begin to meet the demand and the market price will drop. But all this will take time and, during the interval, many more people will be forced to go without eggs than before the government's intervention into the market process.

Any government intervention with the market must proceed in either of two directions. Either the government must return to a free market economy and allow the damages resulting from its intervention to ease gradually, or else the state can keep adding more and more controls until all economic freedom ends. There can be no consistent, successful middle ground between the market and socialism.

One reason interventionist controls fail is that whenever government intervenes in the market, private owners and business people react in ways that spontaneously thwart the objectives of the state. Even worse, when government acts (for example, by restraining price rises) it shuts off important signals that private citizens might otherwise use in making economic decisions. One of the most important features of an unhampered market economy is its informational function. Economic interventionism interferes with the informational function of the market, causes it to send misleading signals, and thus produces significant economic harm.

But interventionists are seldom bothered by little things such as reason and evidence. Whenever confronted by the failures of their partial controls, they have a predictable response. Interventionists argue that previous controls did not go far enough; what is necessary is more interference with the market, not less. In other words, it is always the market process and never interventionism that receives the blame for failure. Through this remarkable sleight of hand, past failures are never regarded as grounds for abandoning interventionism. Rather, the mistakes of the past are used as justification for even more controls in the future. In this way, interventionism tends to move increasingly closer to the total controls of socialism.

As we said earlier, minimum wage laws are a good example of how interventionist policies are counterproductive. Defenders of minimum wage legislation claim that the government must intervene in the market to ensure that employees, especially disadvantaged and unskilled workers, get a "fair" wage. What this interference does, however, is only increase unemployment among those workers whose productivity is too low to justify the minimum rate. Once again, government intervention punishes the very people it was supposed to help.

Liberal arguments that governmental intervention with the economy is necessary to maintain social stability and to enhance freedom and justice are, at best, a cruel joke. Any effort to produce a system of property hampered by government controls will inevitably produce a crisis that must lead either to an abandonment of those partial controls or to a surrender to the total controls of socialism. While partial controls will always result in the interventionist's goals being frustrated, the imposition of total controls would transform the interventionist economy into socialism.[20]

CONCLUSION

It is impossible to understand capitalism until one first distinguishes it from interventionism, the system with which it is often confused. Capitalism is that economic system in which people are encouraged to make voluntary exchanges within a system of rules that prohibit force, fraud, and theft. Interventionism, on the other hand, is that economic system in which powerful people alter the terms of trade in order to benefit some (including themselves, of course) at the expense of others. The American economy is not a capitalist economy; it is an interventionist system.

CHAPTER 5

DOES CAPITALISM PASS THE BIBLICAL TEST?

Because both authors of this book are Christians, we have taken great care to write what is consistent with our Christian worldview. And that means we are concerned with being consistent with the teachings of the Old and New Testaments. In this chapter, we will examine two important passages from the Old Testament that have a direct relevance to the content of this book.

LEVITICUS 25 AND THE JUBILEE YEAR

Almost every Christian liberal or socialist who writes about social justice refers sooner or later, explicitly or implicitly, to the Old Testament notion of the Year of Jubilee in Leviticus 25. Politically liberal Christians claim that the chapter provides God's model for a nation's economy and that the model is basically a socialist view that commands Christians to submit to a coercive government's attempts to redistribute wealth.

Leviticus 25 announces that every fiftieth year in Israel would be a Year of Jubilee. As political liberals read the passage, anyone to whom bad things had happened in the previous forty-nine years would be delivered from their misfortune at the Jubilee. Poor families that had had to sell their land would receive the land back free of charge.

Slaves would be delivered from their bondage.

Ronald Sider, a prominent Christian liberal, once described the Jubilee in these words: "Leviticus is one of the most radical texts in all of Scripture. At least it seems that way for people born in countries committed to either laissez-faire economics [one of Sider's terms for capitalism] or communism. Every fifty years, God said, all land was to return to the original owners—without compensation! Physical handicaps, death of a breadwinner, or lack of natural ability may lead some people to become more poor than others. But God does not want such disadvantages to lead to greater and greater divergence of wealth and poverty. God therefore gave his people a law which would equalize land ownership every fifty years (Lev. 25:10–24)."[21] The truth is that Sider was just plain wrong when he wrote this in 1977. It is interesting to note that some fifteen years later, Sider himself admitted he was wrong.[22]

Stephen Charles Mott, at the time a professor at Gordon-Conwell Divinity School, saw the Jubilee Year as a divine endorsement of a kind of socialist redistribution of wealth.[23] The fact that, under certain conditions, land would revert to the family of the original owners every fifty years could, if read superficially, appear to support the kind of redistribution favored by almost all political liberals. Before that conclusion is asserted dogmatically, the entire chapter should be studied carefully. One should not simply extract from the chapter those verses that appear to support the left-wing position and ignore other verses that suggest something quite different.

A careful examination of Leviticus 25 suggests that Christian liberals give the chapter a highly selective reading. For one thing, the intended redistribution every fifty years did not affect every form of wealth. The only forms of wealth that were affected were slaves[24] and land outside walled cities, such as Jericho and Jerusalem. It is important to note that some land was not affected by the principles of the Jubilee Year. Property sold within walled cities could be redeemed within a year. After the passage of a year, the exchange was regarded as permanent and immune to the changes otherwise affected by the Jubilee (Lev. 25:29–30). Other forms of income, such as fishing boats, were also excluded from the Jubilee practice. While it may be true that land was the most prevalent and important basis of wealth in ancient Israel, the fact that several forms of wealth were excluded from redistribution in the Jubilee is usually slighted in the writings of politically liberal Christian teachers.

It is also true that the Jubilee did not benefit all the poor. For example, it did not help immigrants who had no original inheritance. Moreover, given the relatively short life span of people in those days, the fifty-year interval between Jubilees made it inevitable that many people (those born after one Jubilee who died before the next) were never helped at all. Many who are enthusiastic about the Jubilee concept also forget a vital effect the Jubilee would have had on such economic activity as the buying and selling of land. Had the Jubilee ever been observed (and it never was), it would have ended the buying and selling of land as we know it in favor of leases made more or less valuable by the number of years remaining until the next Jubilee. Under such conditions, anyone contemplating the acquisition of land would know that he was only buying the use of the land for a certain number of years. Land would be most valuable in the first years immediately following a Jubilee and worth relatively little in the years just before a Jubilee.

Most liberal claims about the Jubilee are exaggerated. If its purpose was to encourage and endorse a redistribution of wealth, why were some important forms of wealth unaffected? Why were some of the poor not included? And why was the distribution scheduled at such distant intervals, leaving many people who were born and died between Jubilees without help? Is it important that the Jubilee was never instituted within Israel? Is it relevant that the principles of the Jubilee could not possibly be instituted today, even within Israel?

One of the more surprising elements about the current interest in finding biblical passages that seem to support governmental coercion in redistributing wealth is this: While people exhibit great ingenuity in discovering hitherto unrecognized implications in ambiguous Old Testament passages, hardly anyone bothers to look at several clear texts in the New Testament. Consider just one:

> In the name of the Lord Jesus Christ, we command you, brothers, to keep away from every brother who is idle and does not live according to the teaching you received from us. For you yourselves know how you ought to follow our example. We were not idle when we were with you, nor did we eat anyone's food without paying for it. On the contrary, we worked night and day, laboring and toiling that we would not be a burden to any of you ...For even when we were with you, we gave you this rule: "If a man will not work, he shall not eat." We hear that some among you are idle. They are not busy; they are busybodies. Such people we command and urge in the Lord Jesus Christ to settle down and earn the bread they eat.
>
> —2 THESSALONIANS 3:6–8, 10–12[25]

GENESIS 23 AND ABRAHAM'S PURCHASE OF A GRAVE FOR SARAH

Genesis 23 begins by reporting the death of Abraham's beloved wife, Sarah. After a suitable time of mourning, Abraham begins the sad task of finding and buying the land that will serve as Sarah's grave. As Genesis 23:3–4 states, "Then Abraham rose from beside his dead wife and spoke to the Hittites. He said, 'I am an alien and a stranger among you. Sell me some property for a burial site here so I can bury my dead.'"

After searching for a suitable grave site, Abraham enters into negotiations with a Hittite named Ephron who agrees to sell the land for four hundred shekels of silver. We encourage the reader to study the chapter, for it provides a classic example of what we earlier called "the peaceful means of exchange." Abraham essentially says to Ephron, "If you do something good for me (give me title to the land I desire), then I will do something good for you (give you the money you desire in exchange)." According to Genesis 23:16, "Abraham agreed to Ephron's terms and weighed out for him the price he had named in the hearing of the Hittites: four hundred shekels of silver, according to the weight current among the merchants."

Abraham clearly entered into a free economic exchange that observed the rules mentioned in an earlier chapter: no coercion, no lying, no stealing, and no violation of contracts. Abraham's exchange was clearly what we today would call a capitalist exchange. When God's people in Scripture enter into economic exchanges and behave in God's appointed ways, those exchanges model the peaceful means of exchange. Without question then, capitalism passes the biblical test.

CHAPTER 6

DOES CAPITALISM PASS THE MORAL TEST?

Few people question the economic superiority of capitalism. It works, while socialism does not and indeed cannot. But many critics insist that capitalism must be restricted or even abolished because it allegedly fails important moral tests. We claim, on the contrary, that capitalism is morally superior to socialism.

MORAL OBJECTIONS TO CAPITALISM

Before moral arguments for and against capitalism are presented, it is necessary to eliminate a source of much confusion on this issue. Many critics of capitalism demonstrate they have no idea what capitalism is. The capitalism they attack is a caricature, a straw man. The stereotype of capitalism that is the target of most such attacks often results from an incorrect association of the word *capitalism* with existing national economies that are better described as interventionist. More attention needs to be given to the inappropriateness of regarding the interventionist economic policies of the United States as an instance of capitalism.

Many critics of capitalism appear to be controlled more by emotional hang-ups about capitalism than by actual evidence. Capitalism is blamed for every evil in contemporary society, including its greed, materialism, selfishness, the prevalence of fraudulent behavior, the debasement of society's tastes, the pollution of the environment, the alienation and despair within society and the vast disparities of wealth. Even racism and sexism are treated as effects of capitalism. Many of the objections to a market system result from a simple but clearly fallacious two-step operation. First, some undesirable feature is noted in a society that is allegedly capitalist. Then it is simply asserted without any argument that capitalism is the cause of this feature. Logic texts call this the Fallacy of False Cause. Mere coincidence does not prove causal connection. Such critics of capitalism conveniently overlook the fact that many of these same undesirable features exist in interventionist and socialist systems.

EXPLOITATION

Capitalism is also attacked on the ground that it exploits poor people and poor nations. A crucial but often unstated assumption of this view is the belief that the only way some can become rich is by exploiting others. Poverty is, such critics claim, always the result of exploitation and oppression by someone who profits from the poverty of others.

The exploitation model of poverty is simplistic. It is also an excellent example of the ease with which some extremely confused Christians insist on reading Marxist ideology into the Bible. It is certainly true that Scripture recognizes that poverty sometimes results from oppression and exploitation. But Scripture also teaches that there are times when poverty results from misfortunes that have nothing to do with exploitation. These misfortunes include such things as accidents, injuries and illness. And, of course, the Bible also makes it plain that poverty can result from indigence, sloth and addiction to substances such as alcohol (Prov. 6:6–11; 13:4; 24:30–34; 28:19). When the problem of poverty is approached with a mind unbiased by ideology, it is easy to see that while some poverty does result from exploitation, some does not. Sometimes people are poor because of unforseen circumstances or as a consequence of their own or their family's actions and decisions.

FREE EXCHANGE IS A ZERO-SUM GAME

The myth about exploitation lends support to a related claim that often functions as a ground for rejection of capitalism. Capitalism is denounced because of the mistaken belief that market exchanges are examples of what is called a zero-sum game. A zero-sum game is one wherein only one participant can win. If one person (or group) wins, then the other must lose. Baseball and checkers are two examples of zero-sum games. If A wins, then B must lose.

The error here consists in thinking that market exchanges are a zero-sum game. On the contrary, market exchanges illustrate what is called a positive-sum game—both players may win. We must reject the myth that economic exchanges necessarily benefit only one party at the expense of the other. In voluntary economic exchanges, both parties may leave the exchanges in better economic shape than would otherwise have been the case. Both parties to a voluntary exchange believe that they gain through the trade. If they did not perceive the exchange as beneficial, they would not continue to take part in it.

Capitalism is sometimes despised because it is thought to encourage a number of character traits that are incompatible with Christian values. The two sub-Christian traits most often thought to be encouraged by capitalism are selfishness and greed.

Scripture clearly does condemn selfishness. But the catch is that selfishness should never be confused with the quite different characteristic of self-interest. When Jesus commanded us to love our neighbor as ourself (Matt. 22:39), He gave implicit approval to self-interest. When a person is motivated by selfishness, he seeks his own welfare with no regard for the welfare of others. But when a person is motivated by self-interest, he can pursue his welfare in ways that do not harm others.

There is nothing sinful in caring about what happens to one's family or oneself. In fact, the New Testament condemns those who lack such concern (1 Tim. 5:8). Since the kinds of voluntary exchanges that characterize the market are mutually beneficial (in other words, are a positive-sum game), selfishness is not an inherent feature of capitalism. People who exchange on the basis of market principles engage in activities that benefit themselves and others. The conditions of a free market oblige people to find ways of helping themselves at the same time they help others, whether they do this consciously or not. Self-interest can serve as a powerful engine that pulls society along the road to economic progress.

There is a line beyond which self-interest becomes selfishness. Self-interest means pursuing one's desires in ways that do not detract from the welfare of others. Selfish people pursue their own desires without any regard for the welfare of others. The Bible condones self-interest while condemning selfishness. So too does capitalism when it is understood properly. As Adam Smith wrote in his book, *The Wealth of Nations*, "It is not from the benevolence of the butcher, the brewer, or the baker that we expect our dinner, but from their regard for their own interest. We address ourselves not to their humanity, but to their self-love, and never talk to them of our necessities, but of their advantage."

GREED

Capitalism is also criticized for encouraging greed. However, the mechanism of the market actually neutralizes greed as individuals are forced to find ways of serving the needs of those with whom they wish to exchange. There is no question but that market exchanges often bring us into contact with people motivated by greed. But so long as our rights are protected (a basic condition of market exchanges), the possible greed of others cannot harm us. As long as greedy individuals are prohibited from introducing force, fraud, and theft into the exchange process, their greed must be channeled into the discovery of products or services for which people are willing to trade. Every person in a market economy has to be other-directed. The market is one area of life where concern for the other person is required. The market, therefore, does not pander to greed. It is rather a mechanism that allows natural human desires to be satisfied in a nonviolent way. The alternative to the voluntary means of exchange is coercion.

A MORAL DEFENSE OF CAPITALISM

Many of capitalism's religious critics fail to appreciate that capitalism can be defended not only on the grounds of its economic superiority, but also on moral grounds.

HELP FOR THE MASSES

Critics of capitalism fail to see the extent to which the market process is a force for improving the lot of the masses. History shows that the poor have benefited greatly from market systems. It is impossible to ease, reduce, or eliminate poverty through a continued division of the economic pie into increasingly smaller pieces. There simply is not enough wealth to go around. What the poor of any nation need is not continually smaller pieces of a pie that keeps getting smaller. They need a bigger pie.

Poverty did not begin with capitalism. Capitalism simply made poverty easier to recognize as the poor flocked to urban areas where work was to be found. It also made poverty more noticeable as more members of the middle class rose to modest affluence, making the contrast between them and the poor more apparent.

SOCIAL COOPERATION

Capitalism does more than make it possible for people to make money. It provides the basis for a social structure that encourages the development of important personal and social virtues such as community and cooperation.

PRIVATE OWNERSHIP AND MORAL BEHAVIOR

More attention needs to be given to the important ways in which private ownership can serve as a stimulus to the development of moral behavior. British economist Arthur Shenfield explains:

> Every time we treat property with diligence and care, we learn a lesson in morality...The reason for the moral training of private property is that it induces at least some of its owners to treat it as a trust, even if only for their children or children's

children; and those who so treat it tend to be best at accumulating it, contrary to popular notions about the conspicuous consumption of the rich, the incidence of luck or of gambling. Contrast our attitudes to private property with our treatment of public property. Every army quartermaster, every state school administrator, every bureaucratic office controller, knows with what carelessness and lack of diligence most of us deal with it. This applies everywhere, but especially in socialist countries where most property is public.[26]

Shenfield is right. People do treat their own personal property differently than they treat public property or the property of others. This fact can be used to teach people some important moral lessons.

EVERYTHING HAS A COST

Once people realize that few things in life are free, that most things carry a price tag and that therefore we will have to work for most of the things we want, we are in a position to learn a vital truth about life. Capitalism helps teach this truth. But, Shenfield warns, under socialism, "Everything still has a cost, but everyone is tempted, even urged, to behave as if there is no cost or as if the cost will be borne by somebody else. This is one of the most corrosive effects of [socialism] upon the moral character of people."[27]

Many critics of capitalism focus their attacks on what they take to be its moral shortcomings. In truth, the moral objections to capitalism turn out to be a sorry collection of arguments that reflect, more than anything else, serious confusion about the true nature of a market system. When capitalism is put to the moral test, it more than holds its own against the competition. After all, it makes little sense to reject one system on moral grounds when all of the alternatives turn out, in the real world, to have far more serious problems. To quote Shenfield, among all the economic options, only capitalism "operates on the basis of respect for free, independent, responsible persons. All other systems in varying degrees treat men as less than this. Socialist systems above all treat men as pawns to be moved about by the authorities, or as children to be given what the rulers decide is good for them, or as serfs or slaves. The rulers begin by boasting about their compassion, which in any case is fraudulent, but after a time they drop this pretense which they find unnecessary for the maintenance of power. In all things they act on the presumption that they know best. Therefore they and their systems are morally stunted. Only the free system, the much assailed capitalism, is morally mature."[28]

The alternative to free exchange is coercion and violence. Capitalism is a mechanism that allows natural human desires to be satisfied in a nonviolent way. Little can be done to prevent human beings from wanting to be rich. But what capitalism does is channel that desire into peaceful means that benefit many besides those who wish to improve their own situation.

To quote Shenfield, "The alternative to serving other men's wants is seizing power from them, as it always has been. Hence it is not surprising that wherever the enemies of capitalism have prevailed, the result has been not only the debasement of consumption standards for the masses but also their reduction to serfdom by the new privileged class of Socialist rulers."[29]

Capitalism is quite simply the most moral, most effective, and most equitable system of economic exchange. When capitalism, the system of free economic exchange, is described fairly, there can be no question that it, rather than socialism or interventionism, comes closer to matching the demands of the biblical ethic.

CHAPTER 7

ECONOMICS, MONEY, AND THE CHRISTIAN WORLDVIEW

Many Christians exhibit a schizophrenic attitude toward money and wealth. On the one hand, the necessary role that money plays in enabling people to meet their own basic needs—to say nothing about dispensing charity toward others—obliges us first to earn it and then use it in economic exchange. But on the other hand, many Christians have difficulty reconciling their inescapable involvement with money with biblical passages that seem to contain dire warnings about money, mammon (material wealth regarded as having an evil influence), and wealth. Since "it is easier for a camel to pass through the eye of a needle than for a rich man to enter heaven," they think there must be something dirty and sub-Christian about money. Many Christians approach the topic of money with a feeling of guilt. After all, this world is not supposed to be our home; we are supposed to lay up our treasures in heaven. The world is full of millions of poor and starving people. And yet these Christians have so much in the way of material goods.

Now, of course, there is one obvious way of dealing with all of this. Christians who have more than they need could fulfill what they take to be their Christian duty and give their money away in ways that will help people in need. This requires trust in the integrity and competence of the individuals and agencies who will distribute this donated money. Other Christians who regard their abundance as a trust under God choose to invest excess money in ways that may help others. Too little attention is given to the fact that a Christian who invests in a business is helping others by providing jobs as well as goods and services that people value. When a business is successful, new wealth is created that can benefit an increasing number of people. This is especially true when such investments are made in ways that create jobs and produce useful goods in poor countries.

But a growing number of Christians appear to have little use for the kinds of voluntary measures described in the previous paragraph. Their approach to dealing with those who manage to accumulate more than is required to meet the basic necessities of life involves the use of force. They could choose to educate Christians in the importance of Christian stewardship and encourage them to use their possessions voluntarily in ways that accord with biblical teachings. However, the new class of Christians who support American-style liberalism and the Big Government that goes with it insist that the state use its coercive powers and take whatever it regards as properly excessive and use it in whatever way seems best to the elitists who happen to control the state at that particular time. A new sentiment that controls the thinking of Christian supporters of the Left leads them to claim that money and wealth are somehow evil or at least sub-Christian.

One place where this attitude toward money is apparent is a 1984 book titled *Money and Power* by Jacques Ellul (InterVarsity Press). There is something bizarre about a book that condemns money as evil. One way to see this problem is to ask if Ellul's publisher gave the book away for free and if the translator had done her work without promise of an honorarium (money). As we all know, InterVarsity Press would not have gone to the expense (money) of publishing the book without some expectation of receiving enough money in return to cover more than its costs—something that clear-thinking people call profit. Booksellers would not stock the book without some confidence that customers would be willing to exchange their money for the book.

Ellul's book meshes with a strange mood that has spread through segments of contemporary Christendom. This mood has led many to act as though piety can cover a multitude of intellectual sins. If we are sincere enough and care enough and are pious enough, these people seem to suggest that we can simply ignore the economic and political realities of life.

In still another InterVarsity Press book, Andrew Kirk claims that the Bible teaches that wealth is evil. He writes: "There can be no doubt, if we approach the Bible with honesty, that private accumulation is usually deemed to be the result not of harmless transactions in the market place, but of either violence, fraud, bribes or expropriations..."[30] (Please note that the evil acts cited by Kirk all violate the essence of a genuine free market economy, as noted earlier.) In Kirk's universe, apparently, no one ever prospers honorably. The simple fact that someone possesses more than the bare necessities of life is proof enough for Kirk that the person is defective morally. Kirk supports this indictment of all the people who possess more than Kirk thinks they should by appealing to a number of biblical proof texts. A quick examination of Kirk's proof texts, which include Micah 2:2, Hosea 12:8, and

Jeremiah 5:27–28, will reveal the shallow nature of his biblical exegesis. The verses he cites as proof that all rich people have acquired their holdings dishonestly really say something quite different. Actually, Kirk appeals to texts that condemn the dishonest pursuit of wealth and uses the verses in support of a totally different claim—namely that the Bible condemns all wealth.

WHAT IS MONEY?

Money is first and foremost a medium of exchange. As human society became increasingly more complex, it became inconvenient for humans to barter one commodity or service for another or to exchange a certain quantity of labor for a certain quantity of some commodity. No one invented money; it simply developed. People who wanted to exchange something found that it was sometimes difficult to find someone who had exactly what they wanted and who at the same time wanted exactly what they had to exchange. In order to make exchanges easier, the circle of exchanges widened from two parties to three or more. A had what B wanted; B had what C wanted; C had what A wanted. In this way, indirect exchanges began to develop. Over a period of time, specialized goods that were more difficult to trade were exchanged for goods that were more easily marketed. As a consequence, the more marketable goods became even more marketable because demand for them increased. Eventually, the most marketable or saleable of these goods acquired the function of money, a medium of exchange. Many goods have served as money. In the cultures with which we are most familiar, money tended to take the form of precise weights of such metals as gold and silver.

In this sense of a medium of exchange, money is both a

social and an economic convenience. It makes complicated economic exchanges more convenient and more efficient than if each person had to barter commodities and services directly with other people. Money is an important social institution. A complex society simply could not function without some kind of common medium of exchange. Limitations of time and space do not allow us to explain other important social functions of money.[31]

Given the important social functions of money, it is difficult to understand what Christians such as Jacques Ellul and Andrew Kirk have in mind when they denounce money and wealth. Such Christians seem to have little or no comprehension of what voluntary economic exchange is and how it is a positive-sum game in which both parties can win in the sense of leaving the trade in a better position than they were before the trade. They also seem unaware of the necessary social functions money performs as a medium of exchange, as a measure of value, and as a store of wealth. Much of Ellul's confusion in this area seems to result from his failure to draw a clear distinction between money (anything that may be used as a means of exchange) and mammon (which is money personified as a false god and deified).

MONEY AND MAMMON

Christians such as Ellul are right in warning that money can often assume a sinister power over human lives. But whenever this happens, money (something ethically neutral) has become mammon. When Jesus warned about mammon, He taught that money has the potential of becoming a power that can assume control over people. (See Matthew 6:24; Luke 16:13.) Jesus taught that because humans are sinners, they are capable of turning anything into an idol. Such idols can and often do assume sinister control over the people who treat them as gods. Even though money is a social institution that can be the source of much good, it—like anything else in God's creation—can be turned into an idol. When this happens, money becomes mammon. On the view held by the authors of this book, what should concern believers is not money (something necessary for economic exchange) but improper attitudes toward money.

WHAT DOES THE BIBLE TEACH ABOUT WEALTH?

Claims that the Bible condemns wealth or that God hates all the rich are clearly incompatible with the teachings of Jesus, who saw nothing inherently evil in money, wealth, or private ownership. While Jesus certainly condemned materialism and the compulsive quest for wealth, He never condemned wealth per se. Jesus did not teach that being rich means necessarily being evil.[32] Jesus did not see anything sinful in the ownership of houses, clothes, and other economic goods. He had wealthy friends and followers (Luke 14:1); He stayed in the homes of wealthy people; He ate at their tables (Luke 11:37).

Jesus' teaching stresses human obligations that cannot be fulfilled unless one first has certain financial resources. For example, biblical passages that oblige believers to use their resources for God's purposes presuppose the legitimacy of private ownership.[33] Jesus taught that children have an obligation to care for their parents (Matt. 15:3–9) and that His followers ought to be generous in their support of worthy causes (Matt. 6:2–4). It is rather difficult to fulfill such obligations unless one has certain financial resources.

When Jesus did call on people to renounce their possessions, His statements reflected special conditions; for example, He made this demand in a situation where people had made their possessions into a god (Luke 18:22–24). Instead of condemning wealth, then, Jesus' teaching offered an important perspective on how people living in materialistic surroundings should view the material world. What Jesus condemned was not wealth per se but the improper acquisition and use of wealth. Every Christian, rich or poor, needs to recognize that whatever he or she possesses is theirs temporarily as a steward under God. Wealth that is accumulated dishonestly or that becomes a controlling principle in one's life falls under God's judgment. Wealth resulting from honest labor and wise investment—wealth that is handled by people who recognize their role as stewards under God—does not.

THE WARNING ABOUT MONEY

While there is nothing inherently evil about money or wealth, and while the creation of wealth is a legitimate Christian concern, nevertheless the Bible contains a clear warning that money can and often does have a negative effect on people's character and spiritual relationships. Money can be hazardous to a person's spiritual health. While neither the parable of the rich farmer (Luke 12) nor Lazarus (Luke 16) condemn wealth per se, they illustrate the extent to which the pursuit of wealth can damage a human soul. In Matthew 13:22, wealth was one of the things that choked the growing seed. The rich young ruler could not bring himself to renounce his wealth in order to follow Jesus (Luke 18:18–23). The love of money is the root of all kinds of evil (1 Tim. 6:10).

Without question then, the pursuit of money can

become an obstacle that can make it difficult or even impossible for some to enter the kingdom of God (Mark 10:25). Concern with wealth can encourage the development of such character traits as arrogance, selfishness, self-satisfaction, materialism, and a total indifference to the plight of the needy. Money has the potential of becoming a god that competes for our devotion and commitment.

THE DOCTRINE OF STEWARDSHIP

Humans are only stewards of their possessions. Since God is the Creator of all that exists, He ultimately is the rightful owner of all that exists (Ps. 24:1; Job 41:11). Whatever possessions a human being may acquire, he holds them temporarily as a steward of God and is ultimately accountable to God for how he uses them as well as for how he acquires them. Christians have a duty to use their resources in ways that best serve the objectives of God's kingdom (Matt. 25:24–30; Luke 19:11–27).

The doctrine of stewardship is consistent with the human right to private property. In fact, the biblical norm is not collective or state ownership but private ownership. Many who notice that God ordered the land of Israel to be divided among Jewish families somehow miss the point that this clearly made property rights within Israel private and not public. While the Old Testament views God as the ultimate owner of all that exists, it also teaches that God passed delegated ownership rights on to families.

Unfortunately, the doctrine of Christian stewardship is often misused by Christian Leftists in an attempt to justify the aggrandizement of the state, a necessary step in the implementation of their political ideology. In such a view, the enhancement of social justice requires the transfer of increasing degrees of authority, power, and money to the government, which alone has the compassion and the means to take care of the poor. In this way, Christian stewardship is perverted into a doctrine that obliges Christians to surrender their judgment, will, and resources to the state, which in the view of the Religious Left becomes God's surrogate on earth.[34]

THE OBLIGATION TO SHARE

The followers of Jesus are responsible for those they can help (Matt. 25:31–46). Jesus' disciples were to demonstrate a constant willingness to share their possessions with others (Luke 6:29–30). However, the New Testament says nothing about this sharing being coerced by the state. Once Christians acknowledge their obligation to care about the poor and to take action on behalf of the poor, the next question concerns the best means to do this. Acceptable means in this matter will result in actions and programs that work, not just in the short run, but in the long run. There are certainly times when the poor do require help in the form of cash and noncash benefits in the present, in the short run. But a system of "aid" that encourages people to become dependent on the dole, that robs the poor of any incentive to seek ways of helping themselves, that leads the poor into a poverty trap, is hardly a model of genuine compassion or of wise public policy. Exception must be taken to those Christians who insist that the only approved means of easing poverty is a welfare state, especially when such measures are now known to be so counterproductive.

SUMMARY

The biblical principles we have noted make it clear that Christians are to beware of the enticements of money and wealth. They should beware of allowing their necessary relationship with money to become so important that they fall victim to acquisitiveness, materialism, selfishness, or idolatry. Christians should remember that whatever they have they possess temporarily as stewards of God. They should share with those less fortunate than themselves. But none of this implies that Christians are to shun money and wealth as necessary evils. In spite of the dangers that accompany money and wealth, Christians are called to create wealth and then make certain that they use it in ways that are consistent with their other Christian obligations. It is not how much money you have—it is how much money has you.

CHAPTER

WHAT DOES ECONOMICS HAVE TO DO WITH OUR RELATIONSHIP WITH GOD?

In several important respects, this chapter, the last in our little book, is the most important. During the first part of this chapter, we discuss the important claim that all economic value is subjective. No one can ever understand economics until and unless they grasp this truth. Until this point is mastered, much about human economic activity will remain a mystery. Unfortunately, the first time many religiously inclined people hear this doctrine, they reject it because they believe it is totally inconsistent with important elements of their religious faith. At the appropriate time, we will deal with that objection and show why it is false. Once we have laid the foundation, we will then relate the topic of subjective economic value to important elements of the Christian life.

ALL ECONOMIC VALUE IS SUBJECTIVE

Throughout the history of human thought, a number of important thinkers were led to ponder the question of economic value. Simple observation of how human beings acted in economic exchanges made it clear that some things were thought to have more value than others. What is it about one thing that makes it more valuable than another? Why do people want some goods and services more than others? Why are some things so valued that people are willing to make significant sacrifices in order to obtain them?

Until the late nineteenth century, these earlier attempts to understand the nature and ground of economic value regarded economic value as objective.[35] The value of economic goods was thought to be inherent in some way. Sometime at the end of the nineteenth century, a few economists began to question the objective theory of economic value. These economists argued that economic value is entirely subjective; it exists in the mind of the person who imputes value to the good or service. If something has economic value, it is because someone values it; it is because that good or service satisfies a human want.

One way to see the subjective theory of economic value at work is to go to an auction or a garage sale. Every seller at a garage sale should have learned that the original price of an object is irrelevant to the price it might bring. Be it a pail or a painting, the object is only worth at that moment what some potential buyer is willing to pay for it. Or consider a stamp collector who has asked an auctioneer to sell a beloved collection that represented thousands of work hours and had cost thousands of dollars. There is no way to know ahead of time at what price the collection will finally be hammered down.

Every time human beings make a choice, their decision reflects the subjective value they impute to that resource at that moment. Once you learn this lesson, you will better understand why at one time you choose to read a book and at another time choose to watch a program on The History Channel. You will understand why one day for lunch you go to McDonald's and the next day choose that great Tex-Mex restaurant that's five miles away. All human choices reflect the personal and subjective values we attribute to the options before us at a particular time.

Once economists recognized the personal and subjective ground of economic value, "the science of economics was broadened to encompass all human (purposive/conscious) actions. It became a study of any and all the peaceful (nonviolent) means men use to attain any and all of their various ends..."[36]

These comments contain some important points for Christians to ponder. Christians should welcome the way in which the subjective theory of economic value expanded the horizons of economics to include such concepts as love, honor, friendship, virtue, and help for the less fortunate more than they value such material goods as money, cars, clothes, and houses. Because such people rank love and honor so highly in their personal value scale, their economic choices will reflect this ranking. The conscious purposive actions of such people can be explained by economists who hold to a subjective theory of economic value.

An important qualification must now be made. When economists state that economic value is subjective, they do not restrict the subjective ground of economic value simply to personal tastes. The value that people impute to goods and concepts is also a function of such factors as different knowledge, different interpretations of information, different expectations, and different quantities they already possess. It may also reflect varying degrees of alertness to new opportunities.

People value things differently for a variety of reasons which include: 1) different tastes; 2) different perceptions of available opportunities;[37] 3) different interpretations of other people's actions; 4) different interpretations of current events; 5) different expectations about future events and people's future actions; and 6) different degrees of alertness to previously unrecognized opportunities. Far more is involved in the subjective approach to economic value than personal taste. But what is clear is that economic value is always imputed value; economic value is always subjective.

A THEOLOGICAL OBJECTION

The first time many Christians hear about the subjective theory of economic value, they react negatively because they mistakenly think the theory contradicts important elements of their Christian worldview. "How can I believe that economic values are subjective," they ask, "when as a Christian I am supposed to believe that all value is objective, absolute, and unchanging?" Some Christians believe that an acceptance of the subjective theory we're describing would commit them to believing that all values are relative and subjective. The error in this reasoning should be obvious. Even if we should discover that some values are subjective and relative (such as one's dislike for broccoli or spinach), it would not follow that all values are subjective and relative. The theory that all economic value is subjective in no way obliges anyone to believe that all values are subjective. In no way does our economic theory imply, for example, that ethical values are subjective.

Any number of things, including spiritual conversion, may affect the way people rank things in their personal value scales. To illustrate this, let us imagine a person who realizes he is making bad choices in his life. Perhaps he even knows that his choices are morally wrong. A major part of this person's problem is that his personal scale of values is skewed. Remember that people will always choose the option that ranks highest in their personal scale of values. If that person wants to change his or her conduct, the first thing that must occur is for there to be a major upheaval in his scale of values. But what if we lack the power or ability to change our scale of values?

We have reached a point where an important element of the Christian faith becomes very relevant to our discussion of economics. In some of life's most important matters, there are times when the only thing that can change a person's scale of values, and thus lead to a dramatic change in the way that person lives his or her life, is a spiritual conversion.

The New Testament tells us about a man named Saul. The most important thing in Saul's scale of values was persecuting and killing Christians. Then, quite unexpectedly, Saul of Tarsus met the risen Christ and his life was forever changed. The story of this conversion, this transformation, that forever altered Saul's scale of values is told in chapter 9 of the Book of Acts. After his conversion, Saul's name was changed to Paul. Choices, commitments, and duties that existed nowhere in the preferences of Saul of Tarsus suddenly zoomed to the top of the value scale of the new man, Paul. This is the sort of thing that happens to men and women who have a genuine conversion experience with the living Christ.

CONCLUSION

Our little journey through the strange and often misunderstood world of economics has brought us to a surprising end. The study of a subject that most people think deals primarily with material things such as money and physical possessions turns out to have unexpected consequences for some of the most fundamental moral and spiritual issues in life. We sincerely hope you have learned some important things about economics. But we also would like to think that perhaps you have also learned some new information about yourself, including how important God can be in your life. Our great aim is that we all will experience the freedom that comes as we learn to enjoy being an ennobled Christian steward-servant.

NOTES

1. For examples, see Dr. Ronald H. Nash, *The Closing of the American Heart* (Richardson, TX: Probe Books, 1990).

2. See Dr. Ronald H. Nash, *Poverty and Wealth: Why Socialism Doesn't Work* (Richardson, TX: Probe Books, 1992).

3. See James P. Gills, M.D., and Dr. Ronald H. Nash, *Government Is Too Big* (Tarpon Springs, FL: St. Luke's Cataract and Laser Institute, 1996).

4. For examples, see Nash, *Poverty and Wealth*.

5. See Dr. Ronald H. Nash, *Social Justice and the Christian Church* (Lanham, MD: University Press of America, 1990), chapter 1.

6. Benjamin Rogge, "Christian Economics: Myth or Reality?" *The Freeman*, December 1965.

7. Nash identifies many of these books in his *Social Justice and the Christian Church*, chapter 1.

8. See the first edition of Sider's book, *Rich Christians in an Age of Hunger*, published by InterVarsity Press in 1977. In the most recent edition of this book, Sider has moved away from the Marxism touted in his first book and now says that if Christians want to help the poor, they should become capitalists. See the discussion of Sider's apparent change of mind in Dr. Ronald H. Nash's *Why the Left Is Not Right: The Religious Left: Who They Are and What They Believe* (Grand Rapids, MI: Zondervan, 1996), chapters 7–8. The book is now available only from the author.

9. George Mavrodes, "On Helping the Hungry," *Christianity Today*, December 30, 1977, p. 46.

10. See Charles Murray, *Losing Ground* (New York: Basic Books, 1984); George Gilder, *Wealth and Poverty* (New York: Basic Books, 1981); and Thomas Sowell, *Race and Economics* (New York: David McKay, 1975).

11. James Gwartney, "Social Progress, the Tax-Transfer Society and the Limits of Public Policy," unpublished paper, Department of Economics, Florida State University, p. 3.

12. One of many economists arguing this thesis is Ludwig von Mises. See his book *Human Action*, available in many editions.

13. Nash provides important information about self-described Christian socialists in such books as *Poverty and Wealth: Why Socialism Doesn't Work* and *Why the Left Is Not Right: The Religious Left: Who They Are and What They Believe*.

14. Paul Hollander, *Political Pilgrims* (New York: Oxford University Press, 1981), pp. 416–417.

15. Ibid., p. 417.

16. Our discussion of the problem of economic calculation under socialism must be brief. For much more information, see Nash, *Poverty and Wealth*, chapter 8.

17. Brian Griffiths, *The Creation of Wealth* (Downers Grove, IL: InterVarsity Press, 1985), p. 33.

18. Ibid., p. 26.

19. Significant support for these claims is found in Nash, *Poverty and Wealth*.

20. Our treatment of interventionism is more brief than we would like. For more detail, see Nash, *Poverty and Wealth*, chapter 11.

21. Sider, *Rich Christians in an Age of Hunger*, first edition, p. 88.

22. See Nash, *Why the Left Is Not Right*, chapter 7.

23. See Steven Charles Mott, *Biblical Ethics and Social Change* (New York: Oxford University Press, 1982), chapter 4.

24. Israelites who had been sold into slavery would be freed in the Jubilee. Slaves who were not Israelites would not be freed.

25. See also 1 Thessalonians 4:10–11 and Ephesians 4:28.

26. Arthur Shenfield, "Capitalism Under the Tests of Ethics," *Imprimis*, December 1981.

27. Ibid.

28. Ibid.

29. Ibid.

30. Andrew Kirk, *The Good News of the Kingdom Coming* (Downers Grove, IL: InterVarsity, 1985), p. 71.

31. For this information, see Nash, *Poverty and Wealth*.

32. For the Old Testament view on this subject, see Ecclesiastes 5:19: "Moreover, when God gives any man wealth and possessions, and enables him to enjoy them, to accept his lot and be happy in his work—this is a gift of God."

33. See Luke 16:1–3; 19:11–27; Matthew 25:24–30.

34. For more on this matter, see Nash, *Why the Left Is Not Right*.

35. Actually, there were a few exceptions to the statement in the late Middle Ages, but we do not have time to say more about those thinkers at this time.

36. Bettina Bin Greaves, *Free Market Economics* (Irvington-on-Hudson, NY: Foundation for Economic Education, 1975), p. 173.

37. For example, consider how two prospective investors in a business might reach different decisions because each of them views the opportunities differently.

James P. Gills, M.D., received his medical degree from Duke University Medical Center in 1959. He served his ophthalmology residency at Wilmer Ophthalmological Institute of Johns Hopkins University from 1962–1965. Dr. Gills founded the St. Luke's Cataract and Laser Institute in Tarpon Springs, Florida, and has performed more cataract and lens implant surgeries than any other eye surgeon in the world. Since establishing his Florida practice in 1968, he has

been firmly committed to embracing new technology and perfecting the latest cataract surgery techniques. In 1974, he became the first eye surgeon in the U.S. to dedicate his practice to cataract treatment through the use of intraocular lenses. Dr. Gills has been recognized in Florida and throughout the world for his professional accomplishments and personal commitment to helping others. He has been recognized by the readers of Cataract & Refractive Surgery Today as one of the top 50 cataract and refractive opinion leaders.

As a world-renowned ophthalmologist, Dr. Gills has received innumerable medical and educational awards. In 2005, he was especially honored to receive the Duke Medical Alumni Association's Humanitarian Award. In 2007, he was blessed with a particularly treasured double honor. Dr. Gills was elected to the Johns Hopkins Society of Scholars and was also selected to receive the Distinguished Medical Alumnus Award, the highest honor bestowed by Johns Hopkins School of Medicine. Dr. Gills thereby became the first physician in the country to receive high honors twice in two weeks from the prestigious Johns Hopkins University in Baltimore.

In the years 1994 through 2004, Dr. Gills was listed in The Best Doctors in America. As a clinical professor of ophthalmology at the University of South Florida, he was named one of the best Ophthalmologists in America in 1996 by ophthalmic academic leaders nationwide. He has served on the Board of Directors of the American College of Eye Surgeons, the Board of Visitors at Duke University Medical Center, and the Advisory Board of Wilmer Ophthalmological Institute at Johns Hopkins University. Listed in Marquis' Who's Who in America, Dr. Gills was Entrepreneur of the

Year 1990 for the State of Florida, received the Tampa Bay Business Hall of Fame Award in 1993, and was given the Tampa Bay Ethics Award from the University of Tampa in 1995. In 1996, he was awarded the prestigious Innovators Award by his colleagues in the American Society of Cataract and Refractive Surgeons. In 2000, he was named Philanthropist of the Year by the National Society of Fundraising Executives, was presented with the Florida Enterprise Medal by the Merchants Association of Florida, was named Humanitarian of the Year by the Golda Meir/Kent Jewish Center in Clearwater, and was honored as Free Enterpriser of the Year by the Florida Council on Economic Education. In 2001, The Salvation Army presented Dr. Gills their prestigious "Others Award" in honor of his lifelong commitment to service and caring.

Virginia Polytechnic Institute, Dr. Gills' alma mater, presented their University Distinguished Achievement Award to him in 2003. In that same year, Dr. Gills was appointed by Governor Jeb Bush to the Board of Directors of the Florida Sports Foundation. In 2004, Dr. Gills was invited to join the prestigious Florida Council of 100, an advisory committee reporting directly to the governor on various aspects of Florida's public policy affecting the quality of life and the economic well-being of all Floridians.

While Dr. Gills has many accomplishments and varied interests, his primary focus is to restore physical vision to patients and to bring spiritual enlightenment through his life. Guided by his strong and enduring faith in Jesus Christ, he seeks to encourage and comfort the patients who come to St. Luke's and to share his faith whenever possible. It was through sharing his insights with patients that he initially began writing on Christian topics. An avid student of the Bible for many years, he now has authored nineteen books on Christian living, with over eight million copies in print. With the exception of the Bible, Dr. Gills' books are the most widely requested books in the U.S. prison system. They have been supplied to over two thousand prisons and jails, including every death row facility in the nation. In addition, Dr. Gills has published more than 195 medical articles and has authored or coauthored ten medical reference textbooks. Six of those books were bestsellers at the American Academy of Ophthalmology annual meetings.

As an ultra-distance athlete, Dr. Gills participated in forty-six marathons, including eighteen Boston marathons and fourteen

100-mile mountain runs. In addition, he completed five Ironman Triathlons in Hawaii and holds the record for completing six Double Ironman Triathlons, each within the thirty-six hour maximum time frame. Dr. Gills has served on the National Board of Directors of the Fellowship of Christian Athletes and, in 1991, was the first recipient of their Tom Landry Award. A passionate athlete, surgeon, and scientist, Dr. Gills is also a member of the Explorers Club, a prestigious, multi-disciplinary society dedicated to advancing field research, scientific exploration, and the ideal that it is vital to preserve the instinct to explore.

Married in 1962, Dr. Gills and his wife, Heather, have raised two children, Shea and Pit. Shea Gills Grundy, a former attorney and now full-time mom, is a graduate of Vanderbilt University and Emory Law School. She and her husband, Shane Grundy, M.D., have four children: twins Maggie and Braddock, Jimmy, and Lily Grace. The Gills' son, J. Pit Gills, M.D., ophthalmologist, received his medical degree from Duke University Medical Center and, in 2001, joined the St. Luke's practice. "Dr. Pit" and his wife, Joy, have three children: Pitzer, Parker, and Stokes.

<hr />

Ronald H. Nash, Ph.D., renowned theologian, philosopher, and apologist, went to be with his Lord in March 2006 after a long illness. Dr. Nash taught theology for four decades at three schools. From 1964 to 1991, he served as chairman of the department of philosophy and religion and as the director of graduate studies in humanities at Western Kentucky University. He was a professor at Reformed Theological Seminary from 1991 to 2002 and served  in the same capacity at Southern Baptist Theological Seminary from 1998 to 2005. Dr. Nash wrote more than thirty-five books on theology, philosophy, and apologetics, including *Faith and Reason: Searching for a Rational Faith*; *Life's Ultimate Questions: An Introduction to Philosophy*; *When a Baby Dies*; *Worldviews in Conflict*; *The Word of God and the Mind of Man*; and *Is Jesus the Only Savior?* He had received his undergraduate degree from Barrington College and did post-graduate work at Stanford University. After receiving a master's degree from Brown University, he earned a Ph.D. from Syracuse University. Dr. Nash was a visiting professor at Fullerton Theological Seminary and Trinity Evangelical Divinity School. He had lectured at more than seventy colleges and universities in the United States, as well as at many others in Russia, the Ukraine, Great Britain, Hong Kong, New Zealand, and the Czech Republic. He had also lectured to congressional staff members in the U.S. Capitol Building and had been an advisor to the Civil Rights Commission. Many of Dr. Nash's seminary lectures are available at www.biblicaltraining.org.

R. Albert Mohler, Southern Seminary president, remembers Dr. Nash as a "brilliant and bold defender" of the Christian faith. "He was a man of ideas who believed that right ideas really matter for the preservation of Christ's church. His legacy will endure through his many writings and scores of students."

Russell D. Moore, dean of the School of Theology and senior vice president for academic administration, says, "Ronald Nash was more than just a scholar, more even than just the prolific, influential scholar that he was. He understood that scholarship is a matter of spiritual warfare. Professor Nash didn't simply convey his assertions about the intelligibility and truthfulness of divine revelation or about the exclusivity of the gospel through faith in Christ. He conveyed the gravity and seriousness of the issues for the church."

> We remember with fond appreciation our friend and fellow educator, Ron Nash. It is rare to find such an astute theologian who has an equal grasp of economic theory and practice. Most of all we appreciate his love for the Savior and His truth that shines through all that he penned. May his legacy of writings and lectures equip a new generation with a worldview that takes captive every thought to the obedience of the Redeemer.
>
> —CO-AUTHOR, DR. JAMES P. GILLS

Ludwig von Mises was arguably not only the greatest economist of the twentieth century, but also a genius whose brilliance radiated into other disciplines, including political science, law, and industry. His ideas on war and peace are desperately needed at this time of crisis in America. Mises pointed out that war and welfare are responsible for increasing the size of government to the point where the body of the citizenry cannot support the swollen head of bureaucracy.

The Ludwig von Mises Institute, which is dedicated to promoting his ideas, held a conference that resulted in the publication of a book that calls into question America's foreign policy of interventionism, or being the world policeman. The book is *The Costs of War: America's Pyrrhic Victories*, edited by John V. Denson and published by Transaction Publishers. This book contains numerous essays, all by authors sympathetic to Mises and his ideas. It brings America's military history into clear focus and challenges our current foreign policy of interventionism, which started with the Spanish-American War.

The Mises Institute also has numerous books by Mises or his supporters. These books stress his ideas that parallel those of the founders of America who created a country to be an example to the rest of the world as the ideal for peace and prosperity rather than war and welfare. Mises, as well as America's founders, advocated that peace and prosperity were to be achieved through the free market economy, a limited constitutional government, and a noninterventionist foreign policy.

The Costs of War and other books by and about Ludwig von Mises may be obtained by contacting the Mises Institute at the following address:

Ludwig von Mises Institute
518 West Magnolia Avenue
Auburn, Alabama 36832
334-321-2100
334-321-1111 (fax)
e-mail: mail@mises.org

OTHER BOOKS
by Ronald H. Nash, Ph.D.

Life's Ultimate Questions: An Introduction to Philosophy
Contains information about such great philosophers as Plato, Aristotle, Augustine, and Aquinas, and such topics as arguments for God's existence, the problem of free will, and immortality.
ISBN 0-310-22364-4

Faith and Reason
Contains important information about explaining and defending the Christian worldview, including arguments for God's existence, the problem of evil, and miracles.
ISBN 0-310-29401-0

Worldviews in Conflict
A good introduction to worldview thinking and the Christian worldview in particular.
ISBN 0-310-57771-3

Poverty and Wealth: Why Socialism Doesn't Work
This is Dr. Nash's introduction to economics, strongly recommended by William Simon, former secretary of the U.S. Treasury.
ISBN 0-945-24116-X

Beyond Liberation Theology
This is Dr. Nash's critique of modern attempts to link Christianity and Marxism.
ISBN 0-80101-022-5

The Closing of the American Heart: What's Really Wrong With America's Schools
Contains important information about what's wrong with America's public schools and universities. An important book for parents of school-age and college students.
ISBN 0-945-24111-9

Is Jesus the Only Savior?
How and why many contemporary Christian leaders are denying that Jesus is the only Savior.
ISBN 0-310-44391-1

When a Baby Dies
When children die in infancy or when babies die before birth, are they saved? How are they saved if they cannot believe? Questions about heaven.
ISBN 0-310-22556-6

The Meaning of History
How does the Christian view of history differ from secular theories? Is there meaning to history? What is that meaning?
ISBN 0-805-41400-2

Why the Left Is Not Right: The Religious Left:
Who They Are and What They Believe
Dr. Nash's answers to socialists in the church.

ISBN 0-310-21015-1

Great Divides: Ten Controversies That Come Between
Christians
Covers such issues as abortion, political liberalism, radical feminism, psychological counseling, and biblical prophecy.

ISBN 0-891-09696-5

Many of Dr. Nash's books are available via the internet at www .amazon.com or www.barnesandnoble.com.

THE WRITINGS OF
James P. Gills, M.D.

A Biblical Economics Manifesto
(With Ron H. Nash, Ph.D.)
The best understanding of economics aligns with what the Bible teaches on the subject.

ISBN: 978-0-88419-871-0   E-book ISBN: 978-1-59979-925-4

Believe and Rejoice: Changed by Faith, Filled With Joy
Observe how faith in God can let us see His heart of joy.

ISBN: 978-1-59979-169-2   E-book ISBN: 978-1-61638-727-3

Come Unto Me: God's Call to Intimacy
Inspired by Dr. Gills' trip to Mt. Sinai, this book explores God's eternal desire for mankind to know Him intimately.

ISBN: 978-1-59185-214-8   E-book ISBN: 978-1-61638-728-0

Darwinism Under the Microscope: How Recent Scientific
Evidence Points to Divine Design
(With Tom Woodward, PhD)
Behold the wonder of it all! The facts glorify our Intelligent Creator!

ISBN: 978-0-88419-925-0   E-book ISBN: 978-1-59979-882-0

The Dynamics of Worship
Designed to rekindle a passionate love for God, this book gives who, what, where, when, why, and how of worship

ISBN: 978-1-59185-657-3   E-book ISBN: 978-1-61638-725-9

Exceeding Gratitude for the Creator's Plan: Discover the
Life-Changing Dynamic of Appreciation
Standing in awe of the creation and being secure in the knowledge of our heavenly hope, the thankful believer abounds in appreciation for the Creator's wondrous plan.

ISBN: 978-1-59979-155-5   (Hardcover) ISBN: 978-1-59979-162-3
E-book ISBN: 978-1-61638-729-7

God's Prescription for Healing: Five Divine Gifts of Healing
Explore the wonders of healing by design, now and forevermore.
ISBN: 978-1-59185-286-5   (Hardcover) ISBN: 978-0-88419-947-2
E-book ISBN: 978-1-61638-730-3

Imaginations: More Than You Think
Focusing our thoughts will help us grow closer to God.
ISBN: 978-1-59185-609-2   E-book ISBN: 978-1-59979-883-7

Love: Fulfilling the Ultimate Quest
Enjoy a quick refresher course on the meaning and method of God's great gift.
ISBN: 978-1-59979-235-4   E-book ISBN: 978-1-61638-731-7

Overcoming Spiritual Blindness
Jesus + anything = nothing. Jesus + nothing = everything. Here is a book that will help you recognize the many facets of spiritual blindness as you seek to fulfill the Lord's plan for your life.
ISBN: 978-1-59185-607-8   E-book ISBN: 978-1-59979-884-4

Resting in His Redemption
We were created for communion with God. Discover how to rest in His redemption and enjoy a life of divine peace.
ISBN: 978-1-61638-349-7   E-book ISBN: 978-1-61638-425-8

Rx for Worry: A Thankful Heart
Trust your future to the God who is in eternal control.
ISBN: 978-1-59979-090-9   E-book ISBN: 978-1-59979-926-1

The Prayerful Spirit: Passion for God, Compassion for People
Dr. Gills tells how prayer has changed his life as well as the lives of patients and other doctors. It will change your life also!
ISBN: 978-1-59185-215-5   E-book ISBN: 978-1-61638-732-7

The Unseen Essential: A Story for Our Troubled Times
Part One
This compelling, contemporary novel portrays one man's transformation through the power of God's love.
ISBN: 978-1-59185-810-2   E-book ISBN: 978-1-59979-513-3

Tender Journey: A Story for Our Troubled Times
Part Two
Be enriched by the popular sequel to The Unseen Essential.
ISBN: 978-1-59185-809-6   E-book ISBN: 978-1-59979-509-6

The Worry Disease
This colorful pamphlet teaches how to banish worry by trusting in God and thanking Him always!
Pamphlet

DID YOU ENJOY THIS BOOK?

We at Love Press would be pleased to hear from you if

A Biblical ECONOMICS Manifesto

has had an effect on your life or the lives of
your loved ones.

Send your letters to:

Love Press
PO Box 5000
Tarpon Springs, FL 34688-5000